M000092733

This Notebook Belongs To

____

Copyright © HappyHappyJournaling

Made in the USA
Monee, IL
08 August 2021

75201117R00070